THE FREEDOM OF RELIGION IN AMERICA

The IN AMERICA *Series*

THE FREEDOM OF RELIGION
IN AMERICA

RAVINA GELFAND

Published by
Lerner Publications Company
Minneapolis, Minnesota

Copyright © 1969 by Lerner Publications Company

All rights reserved — no part of this book may be reproduced in any form without permission in writing from the publisher, except for the inclusion of brief quotations in a review.

International Copyright Secured. Printed in U.S.A.
Standard Book Number: 8225-0219-4
Library of Congress Catalog Card Number: 68-31502

Second Printing 1969
Third Printing 1972

...CONTENTS...

PART I.
1. *The Freedoms to Worship and Believe* 8
2. *Religious Practices—The Freedom to Act* 8
3. *The Debate Today* 12
4. *A Closer Look at the First Amendment* 13
5. *What Is an Establishment of Religion?* 13
6. *Government and Public Opinion* 14

PART II. Intolerance in Colonial America
1. *Virginia* 15
2. *The Puritans in Massachusetts* 16
3. *Conditions in Other Colonies* 18

PART III. First Attempts to Achieve Tolerance
1. *Maryland* 19
2. *The Livelie Experiment* 22
3. *The Quakers and William Penn* 26

PART IV. The Growth of Religious Freedom
1. *The Increased Colonial Population* 31
2. *Freedom and Economics* 32
3. *The Spread of New Ideas* 33
4. *Freedom for a Free Nation* 34

PART V. Heroes, Liberty of Conscience, and Constitutions
1. *Virginia—The Model for Religious Freedom* 35
2. *The Constitution of the United States* 40
3. *Guarantees by the States* 42

PART VI. A New Era Begins
1. *Protection of Religious Freedom Extended* 43
2. *How the Supreme Court Operates* 44

PART VII. The Supreme Court Studies the Free Exercise of Religion
1. *Religion and Law—An Early Opinion* 45
2. *Religion and Law—The Current Opinion* 47
3. *Compulsory Flag Salute* 47
4. *What Is a Religion?* 50
5. *Claims of Religious Experiences* 53
6. *Religious Requirements for Public Officeholding* 55
7. *Free Exercise of Religion—How the Court Determines Limits* 55

PART VIII. The Supreme Court Studies the Establishment Clause
1. *What Does the Establishment of Religion Clause Mean?* 57
2. *An Establishment of Religion—How the Court Decides* 58
3. *Why Does the Court Say "Government Can Not Aid Religion"?* .. 59
4. *The Argument for Government Aid to Religion or Religious Schools* 60
5. *Disagreement Among Supreme Court Justices* 60

PART IX. Aid to Parochial School Children
1. *The New Jersey Bus Fare Case* 61
2. *Textbook Loans to Parochial School Children* 64

PART X. Religious Instruction During Public School Hours
1. *Released Time for Religious Instruction in a Public School* 66
2. *Released Time for Religious Instruction Given Outside the School* 67

PART XI. Prayer and Bible Reading in Public Schools
1. *The New York Regents' Prayer Case* 71
2. *Daily Bible Reading and Recitation of the Lord's Prayer* 74
3. *Reaction to the Court's Ban on Religious Exercises in Public Schools* 77
4. *Attempts to Change the First Amendment* 78
5. *Public Opinion After 1964* 78
6. *Church and State—The Court's Dilemma* 80

PART XII. Conclusion
1. *The Free Exercise of Religion* 81
2. *An Establishment of Religion* 82

Pilgrim couple going to worship. Strong in their opposition to the Church of England, the Pilgrims chose to separate from the Church and move to Holland where they expected to worship more freely. In 1620, they traveled to America and founded the Plymouth Colony as their exclusive religious community.

Public whipping of a Quaker in the London Sessions House yard, 1745.

PART I

> Congress shall make no law respecting an establishment of religion, or prohibiting the free exercise thereof; or abridging the freedom of speech, or of the press; or the right of the people peaceably to assemble, and to petition the Government for a redress of grievances.—*Amendment I, The Constitution of the United States*

The first words of the First Amendment to the Constitution of the United States guarantee to Americans their prized liberty of freedom of religion. This freedom came after centuries of persecution. Catholics had persecuted Protestants; Protestants had persecuted Catholics; and both groups had persecuted Jews, atheists, doubters, and even persons of their own faith who were not worshipping in the manner demanded by whoever happened to be in power. Often the persecuted people were required to help support the churches whose members were persecuting them.

In 1791, when the First Amendment was adopted, it protected religious freedom from being violated by laws passed by the Federal Government only. With the passage of a later amendment, and through opinions of the Supreme Court, the protection offered was enlarged to include laws passed by the states.

Persecution of Jews. In 1614, Vincenz Fettmilch led an attack on the Jewish ghetto of Frankfort-am-Main, Germany. A massacre and book-burning followed the conflict.

1. *The Freedoms to Worship and Believe*

Under the constitutional protection of religious freedom, the liberties to worship and believe are absolute, that is, there are no circumstances under which government can take them away. No law can demand that we accept any one religion or any religion at all. No law can prevent us from believing in any religion we choose. No law can force us to attend a house of worship. Nor can any law keep us from attending a house of worship. No one can be required to hold any particular religious belief, or any religious belief at all, in order to hold public office or work for a branch of government.

2. *Religious Practices — The Freedom to Act*

Some religious rights are not always absolute. These involve religious practices — actions that our religions require of us or forbid us from taking. Religious practices may be prohibited if they violate laws, disturb the peace, or are harmful to the welfare of an individual or society.

A problem arises, for example, in cases of persons whose religious beliefs do not permit medical treatment. Most state courts have ruled that it is legal for the state to order treatment, against the wishes of parents, if the treatment is necessary to save the life of a child. When an adult refuses medical treatment for himself, a court will rarely interfere.

The education of Mennonite Amish children has caused several states to face the complicated questions which arise when religious practices are contrary to law.

The Amish religion teaches that modern ways should not be adopted. In communities modeled according to this belief, inventions such as automobiles, television sets, radios, and telephones are not used. The children learn such subjects as reading, writing, and arithmetic. They are also taught farming, homemaking, and religious values to equip them for a useful life among their own people.

Amish parents do not want their children to attend public schools where they will study subjects (such as science) which may give them ideas different from those stressed by their religion. They feel that an eighth grade education is all that a child or his teacher should have.

Most state laws require children to attend school until they are 16. They also require teachers to have special education which qualifies them to teach. These rules were made for the protection and well-being of children. But when state officials force the Amish to obey the laws, they are violating Amish religious freedom.

Amish boy preparing to harrow the fields. Since modern ways are shunned in Amish society, the horse remains the major means of pulling farm equipment.

Amish children singing in school. Amish parents prefer their own schools to the public schools because they do not want their children to learn ideas that might conflict with those of the Amish religion.

Because parents who do not keep their children in state-approved schools can be fined or sentenced to prison, the Amish have been involved in many court battles.

A number of states have made special efforts to protect Amish religious freedom. Iowa children may be exempt from school requirement laws which conflict with their religious beliefs. This means that the Iowa Amish can legally keep their children out of school after the eighth grade and can use teachers who have had no more than an eighth grade education. Other states have stretched existing laws so that Amish children may be educated in a way which can be considered legal and, at the same time, acceptable to their parents. However, in some states the arrest and fining of Amish parents has forced them to send their children to public schools.

While religious practices are sometimes restricted, they are more often protected. Our government is concerned with protecting religious practices even when the rights of a small minority are involved. When a number of Amish farmers refused to pay Social Security taxes, claiming that this insurance denies faith in God, Congress granted them the right not to take part in the Social Security program. A Supreme Court ruling forbids a state to deny unemployment compensation to anyone who loses his job because his religion forbids him to work on his Sabbath. People whose religious principles require them not to judge the actions of others may be excused from jury duty.

Amish children at recess. Because the Amish school standard differs from that of the public schools, demands have been made that Mennonite parents send their children to the public schools. Many feel that this imposes on their religious freedom.

A Jewish boy reads from the Torah. Jewish history is filled with instances of persecution, from forced ghetto settlement to mass extermination. In America, for the first time, Jews were granted full liberties and allowed complete freedom of worship.

3. *The Debate Today*

Our right to believe or not believe, to attend any house of worship or no house of worship, is secure. Our right to act according to the requirements of our religion is secure unless those actions violate the law, disturb the peace, or are harmful to an individual or society.

Still, religious freedom is the topic of constant debate in books, magazines, meeting rooms, and court rooms.

Should pupils attending church-operated schools be provided transportation at public expense? Should churches pay taxes? Should public school children be excused from classes to take religious training?

These are a few of the questions on which American opinion is divided.

4. *A Closer Look at the First Amendment*

Many people wonder why religious freedom has suddenly become the subject of so much controversy. To the average American, freedom of religion means the right to worship, believe, and observe religious practices. This is the guarantee of the free exercise of religion written into the First Amendment. This part of the Amendment is often called the *Free Exercise Clause.* But the First Amendment says more than that. It also states that Congress shall make no law respecting an establishment of religion. This part of the amendment, known as the *Establishment Clause,* forms the basis for most of the current disagreement.

5. *What Is an Establishment of Religion?*

In seventeenth-century America most colonies had "established churches." These churches were part of government—built by order of the colonial governments with tax money collected from all residents of the colony. Tax money was also used to maintain the churches and to pay the ministers' salaries. Only the churches of one denomination could be built, and members of other denominations were persecuted when they tried to worship according to their own beliefs. In some colonies the government controlled the church. In other colonies the church controlled the government.

An official government church is the most obvious illustration of an establishment of religion. Americans eventually learned that separation of Church and State (separation of religion and government) was necessary for the protection of the church, the state, and the individual.

Do the words "Congress shall make no law respecting an establishment of religion" mean only that there should be no official government church? Most people agree that they do not. Most people also agree that there is an establishment of religion any time religion becomes too much a part of the business of government. The disagreement occurs over the question of what kinds of government action make religion too much a part of the business of government.

6. *Government and Public Opinion*

Our government can only be government by the people if the people make their opinions known. Each of us has many opportunities to do this. Adults and young people alike may belong to political organizations, be active in civic groups, write to government officials, and work to help political candidates whose views they understand and approve of. Our history shows that the actions of our nation's lawmakers are usually guided by the wishes of the people.

In a society where public opinion can play such an important part in governing the lives of its citizens, it is essential that any stand on public issues be based on careful thought and understanding.

Religious freedom becomes a public issue almost every time the use of tax money has any effect on religion or religious institutions. It also becomes a public issue when government officials have to choose between their duty to enforce a particular law and their duty to protect the free exercise of religion.

These issues can be best understood by learning about some of the events in American history which led to the guarantees of freedom of worship and separation of Church and State. A study of representative court decisions will illustrate how our judges interpret the meaning of religious liberty. With this background the reader can begin to form an opinion about the kind of relationship between government and religion that will best guard our religious freedom.

NOTICE:
TO ALL HERRICKS SCHOOL DISTRICT TAXPAYERS
A taxpayers suit will soon be started to challenge the legality of prayers in public schools counsel has been appointed.
All interested parties CALL:
LAWRENCE ROTH
MAYFAIR 1 – 7652 AFTER 5 P.M., DAILY

A taxpayer's suit is initiated when a citizen, as a taxpayer, feels that he is being harmed by a state ruling. In 1958, Lawrence Roth wanted to challenge the legality of prayers in the public schools. He inserted an ad in two Long Island newspapers and received a good response, finally choosing five persons to work with him — two Jews, one Unitarian, one member of the Ethical Culture Union, and one nonbeliever.

St. Luke's Church, Smithfield, Virginia. Built in 1632, it is the oldest remaining church in America and stands as a national shrine.

PART II

Intolerance in Colonial America

1. *Virginia*

Church and State in colonial America were linked together from the time of the founding of Virginia, the first permanently settled English colony. The Virginia founders came to America in search of economic opportunities. They admired the English way of life and planned to duplicate it in their colonial community. It seemed only natural to them to establish the Church of England (Protestant Episcopal) as Virginia's official church. All residents of Virginia, whether or not they were Episcopalian, were taxed to build and to support Episcopal churches and to pay the salaries of their ministers. Dissenters (people who did not agree with the teachings of the established church) were not allowed to build churches of their own. Severe Virginia laws were used whenever authorities felt they were needed to keep dissenting sects from gaining strength in the colony. Thus, at times during the history of the colony, Puritans and Quakers were barred. At times Catholics were not permitted to hold public office, vote, or worship in public. And, more than 150 years after the colony was founded, a number of Baptists preachers were whipped and imprisoned.

2. *The Puritans in Massachusetts*

The strongest of the New England colonies was founded in 1629 by the Puritans who settled in and around Boston in the Massachusetts Bay area. There they established the Congregational Church. It was part of the church system of the Church of England, but had been changed to do away with what the Puritans considered the sinful practices of the English Church.

In Massachusetts Bay the Puritans worked to create "a heavenly city of God" where the Bible provided the rules for living. This kind of society could exist only if the "right" people belonged to the church and governed the community. Those who wanted to be church members were thoroughly questioned about their religious experiences, their beliefs, and the way they lived. Many were not allowed to join the church because their answers weren't approved. Since only church members could vote, the colony was governed by a small minority.

John Winthrop (1588-1649) and **John Cotton** (1584-1652). Winthrop, governor of the Massachusetts Bay Colony, was opposed to a broad democracy. He helped to shape the Colony's system which gave clergymen great authority over the citizens. John Cotton, a Puritan minister in the Colony, worked with Winthrop to oppose all dissenters and critics of the Colony's established church.

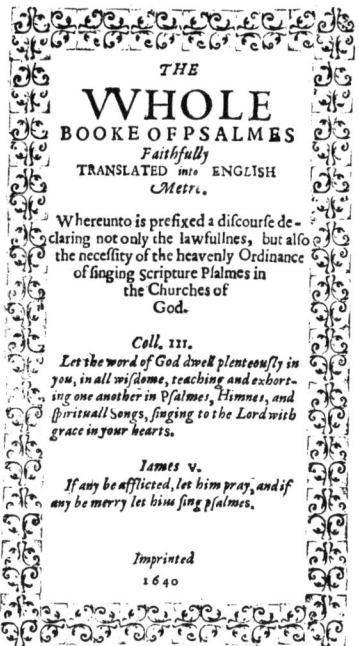

The Bay Psalm Book of 1640, common hymnal of the Massachusetts Bay Colony. It was the first book printed in the United States.

Some Massachusetts Bay colonists had no desire to pass the religious tests because the lives of church members were so strictly regulated. Living by the Bible included every aspect of life—political thinking, business activities, and recreation. It dictated what clothing could be worn and how parents should educate their children. Church members not attending Sunday prayer meeting had to have a good excuse or be punished. Even an expression of gaiety on a Sunday brought disapproval.

In order to prove that a community governed by the Bible would produce a superior way of life, all Puritans had to believe and live the same way. There could be no criticism of the church and no outside influences on its members. When the first Quakers arrived in 1655 they were whipped, imprisoned, and then sent away from the colony. When these measures failed to keep Quakers from coming to Massachusetts Bay, a law was passed which provided for the hanging of any banished Quaker who returned. Catholic priests were also banned under threat of death. Baptists were, at times, whipped and imprisoned.

Intolerance spread from Massachusetts Bay to nearby Plymouth. That colony, founded in 1620, had not at first required church membership as a condition for voting, and the first settlers were not taxed to support the church. By the middle of the century, however, religious freedom in Plymouth was as restricted as in Massachusetts Bay.

3. Conditions in Other Colonies

Although the degree of intolerance differed from one colony to another, not one of them was completely free of intolerance at all times.

The majority of the colonies either started out with, or eventually established, state-churches. Rhode Island, Pennsylvania, and Delaware (which was governed as part of Pennsylvania for many years) never had an established church. New Jersey had official connections with the Church of England, but historians do not agree on whether or not the colony had an established church.

After England passed a Toleration Act in 1689 there was a gradual improvement of conditions for persecuted Protestants in America. At the same time Catholics in most colonies lost what freedom they had.

Pilgrims going to church. The first Pilgrims had not demanded church membership and church support from all the citizens. This restriction on religious freedom came later in the seventeenth century. No colony was completely free from intolerance.

The founding of Maryland, 1634. George Calvert was granted the first deed to Maryland, but he died before the charter could be accepted. It was his son, Cecil, who undertook the real task of settlement.

PART III

First Attempts to Achieve Tolerance

1. *Maryland*

In the early seventeenth century there was little opportunity for Catholics in England or America to practice their religion openly. In 1634 Cecil Calvert founded the colony of Maryland, partly as a business venture and partly to provide a place where Catholics could worship in peace.

To attract settlers, and to keep the good will of the Protestant English government, Calvert guaranteed religious freedom to Protestants and Catholics alike. In 1636 he drew up an oath to be taken by all Maryland governors. The oath promised punishment for anyone who would molest a Christian because of his religion.

Distrust of Catholics caused problems in Maryland from the colony's earliest years. Cecil Calvert had to remain in England in order to make quick appeals for government help each time an emergency arose. He governed Maryland through instructions given to members of his family and other representatives living in the colony. In spite of all efforts to please Maryland Protestants,

Cecil Calvert (1605-1675), founder of Maryland, never visited the colony himself. He governed it through deputies from 1634 until his death.

they complained to the British government that Catholics dominated the colony. In fear of losing his charter, Calvert, in 1648, appointed a Protestant, William Stone, as Governor of Maryland. Stone immediately invited several hundred Virginia Puritans to move to Maryland where they would be allowed to vote and to worship freely. Soon they, too, were opposing Calvert's rights to the colony.

Cecil Calvert then drafted the Maryland Act concerning Religion, also known as the Maryland Toleration Act. The Act was intended to protect Catholics and to reassure Protestants who feared living in a colony whose charter was held by a Catholic.

Calvert's Act granted complete freedom of worship to all who believed in Jesus Christ, but the Protestants in the Maryland Assembly amended it to eliminate Unitarians from the guarantee. Anyone who expressed disbelief in the Holy Trinity, or who said that Jesus Christ was not the son of God, was to be executed. The Act also provided for whipping, fines, or imprisonment for anyone who called another person a name suggesting disrespect of his religion or for undignified action on Sunday.

The Maryland Act concerning Religion was not a guarantee of religious freedom as we think of it today. Nevertheless, it permitted the majority of Christians to live as neighbors and worship in their own churches — a large step forward for the times.

By 1649, when the Maryland Toleration Act was passed, Puritans were in power in England. Within five years Maryland, too, was controlled by Puritans. No longer able to get support from the English government, Cecil Calvert lost his colonial charter. Catholics in Maryland were denied the right to vote, and the Act concerning Religion was repealed.

In only four years the make-up of England's government changed again and Calvert's colonial rights were restored. Under his leadership the Toleration Act was once more put into effect.

This time Catholics in Maryland managed to hold on to their religious freedom for almost 30 years. During that period the Duke of York, a convert to Catholicism, used his influence to help American and English Catholics. He became England's King James II in 1685, but was soon overthrown because of his efforts in behalf of Catholicism. With no influence in the English government, the Calvert family's attempt to grant freedom of worship to all Christians in colonial Maryland ended a failure. The Church of England became the established church of Maryland. Catholics again were not allowed to worship in public, and Catholic immigrants were forbidden to come to the colony to live.

James II (1633-1701) ruled England from 1685 to 1688. As a convert to Catholicism, he supported the Catholic cause in both England and America.

Roger Williams (1603-1683), founder of Rhode Island, was a strong defender of religious freedom.

2. *The Livelie Experiment*

While the Calverts were settling Maryland, events were taking place in Massachusetts which would lead to the founding of the first colony in America to grant full religious freedom. These events began in 1631 with the arrival in Boston of Roger Williams.

Williams was given a warm welcome when he came from England to Massachusetts Bay. He was a minister, and ministers were greatly needed by the Puritans. But the welcome became cooler when Williams refused an invitation to be a pastor in Boston. The Puritan church, he said, by not completely separating from the Church of England, was a religion where the unholy worshipped with the holy and the ungodly with the godly. He wanted to preach to a pure church — a church made up of true believers only.

In a community where criticism of the church was not allowed, Williams's behavior was considered shocking. He was young, however, and for a while the leaders of the church-state put up with him, hoping he would recognize the errors of his "strange" ideas.

Instead, having already criticized the church, Williams went on to criticize the government. Basing his arguments on the Bible, he protested against the Massachusetts system under which public officials handled much of the church business and the punishment of persons who violated church rules. "The civil magistrates power extends only to the bodies and goods and outward state of men," Williams declared. Government could enforce laws dealing with men's actions and property so long as those laws had nothing to do with religious beliefs. Williams was arguing for separation of Church and State more than 150 years before the idea became an accepted American principle.

Williams did preach at some Massachusetts churches, but their connection with the Church of England disturbed him greatly. In 1634 he asked his congregation in Salem to renounce the other New England churches and form a church where only true believers would worship.

Puritan authorities, already enraged by Williams, could tolerate him no longer. They collected letters he had written, took testimony on the ideas he had preached, and brought him to trial in 1635. The result was the decree by the General Court that:

> Whereas, Mr. Roger Williams...hath broached and divulged divers new and dangerous opinions, against the authority of magistrates; hath also writ letters of defamation, both of the magistrates and churches here...Mr. Williams shall depart out of this jurisdiction...not to return any more without license from the Court.

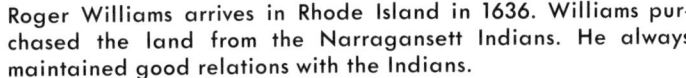

Roger Williams arrives in Rhode Island in 1636. Williams purchased the land from the Narragansett Indians. He always maintained good relations with the Indians.

Settlement of Rhode Island.

To avoid being sent back to England, Williams fled from Massachusetts. After wandering in the wilderness for 14 weeks, he settled on land which he purchased from the Indians. There he founded the settlement of Providence, which eventually joined with neighboring settlements to become Rhode Island.

In Providence, Roger Williams began a community where people of all faiths were welcome. The man who had once declared that he would preach only in a pure church to true believers was now willing to preach to anyone. He had come to realize that no one could know if a church was really pure and who was really a true believer.

A large number of Baptists came to Rhode Island. It was an ideal place for them to live, for of all the sects then in America, the Baptists were the most outspoken in their belief in separation of Church and State. Here they could see their principle at work.

Quakers, Jews, and others who had not been allowed to worship freely anywhere in the English-speaking world, also came to Rhode Island to live.

Roger Williams became a Baptist for a short time. After that he called himself a Seeker — he was looking for the truth in religion, but did not recognize any one church. He made no exception in his belief in equal rights for everyone. Although he personally felt strong disagreement with the teachings of the Quakers, he insisted that they have the right to worship, to vote, and to hold public office. Other New England colonies warned that there would be no trade or any other dealings between themselves and Rhode Island if the colony didn't pass anti-Quaker laws. But the people of Rhode Island said they would have no laws to punish people because of their religious beliefs.

When it became necessary, because of changes in the English government, to obtain a new charter for Rhode Island, the colony's citizens made it clear that they wished to continue their policy of religious freedom. Their wishes were expressed by the Baptist preacher, John Clarke, whose petition to the King stated that the people desired "to be permitted to hold forth in a livelie experiment that a most flourishing Civill State may stand, yea, and best be maintained...with full libertie of religious concernments."

Second Baptist Meetinghouse. In 1639 Roger Williams and his associates organized a Baptist church in Rhode Island. The first meetinghouse was built in 1700 at the personal expense of the pastor. It was deeded to the Church in 1711. The second meetinghouse, built in 1774-1775, is still used for commencement exercises by Brown University.

The new charter was granted in 1663. It went further in its guarantee of religious liberty than any ever written when it declared:

> ...that noe person within the sayd colonye, at any tyme hereafter, shall bee any wise molested, punished, disquieted, or called in question, for any difference in opinione in matters of religion which doe not actually disturb the civill peace...but that all and everye person...at all tymes hereafter, freelye and fullye have and enjoye his and their own judgments and consciences, in matters of religious concernments....

After the death of Roger Williams, in 1683, there was some loss of freedom in Rhode Island. Laws were passed which limited citizenship and eligibility to public office to Protestants. But the influence of Roger Williams, John Clarke, and other early settlers remained with the Rhode Island colonists. These new laws were not strictly observed, and they ceased to be observed at all long before they were repealed. Rhode Island stood as an example to Americans that a civil state could flourish while granting full religious freedom.

3. *The Quakers and William Penn*

The Society of Friends, commonly called the Quakers, were persecuted from the time the movement was started by George Fox in 1647.

Following their religious beliefs made life difficult for Quakers in the seventeenth century. They did not believe in taking oaths, and most governments required a pledge of loyalty from their citizens. They were against war and would not carry arms, and governments did not trust anyone who would not promise to defend them. They were ridiculed because they would not remove their hats to anyone, even to royalty, believing that only God deserved this mark of respect. During periods when minorities were subject to extreme punishment, some sects hid their views, but the Quakers refused to go into hiding.

The cruel treatment of Quakers, intended to discourage their activities, had the opposite effect. Some Quakers considered it an

George Fox preaching in a tavern. In 1646, Fox had a mystical experience which taught him that God was in the soul of every man and no man needed a particular religious creed to bind him. He began preaching his beliefs in his native England, establishing the Society of Friends in 1647. To further spread his ideas, Fox traveled to America in 1671. He and his followers were subjected to many forms of persecution, especially to public whippings. There was great dislike for Quaker doctrine and for the Quakers' uncompromising loyalty to their religion.

William Penn (1644-1718), founder of Pennsylvania, spent his life supporting the cause of religious freedom. Imprisonment did not stop him from writing pamphlets and debating his point of view.

honor to suffer for their religion and purposely went to preach where they were most persecuted.

Many who witnessed Quaker fearlessness in the face of imprisonment and torture came to admire them. Some people listened carefully to what they were preaching and converted to their cause. Such a man was William Penn.

Penn had been brought up as a member of the Church of England. As the son of wealthy and influential parents he enjoyed privileges unknown to most Englishmen. Yet, even as a young boy, he was dissatisfied with the injustices he saw around him. He became attracted to Quaker teachings while still in his teens. At 23 he made the final break from his family's traditions to become a member of the Society of Friends.

After becoming a Quaker, William Penn devoted most of his time to giving speeches, participating in debates, and writing letters and pamphlets for the cause of his religion. He believed that Quaker ideals were best, but he accepted and worked to spread the Quaker principle that every man had the right to worship according to his conscience. His activities landed him in jail several times, but, like other Quakers, imprisonment did not discourage him.

In 1677, after Penn and other Quakers had obtained colonial rights to land in New Jersey, he helped form a plan of government for West Jersey, America's first Quaker colony. The West Jersey plan stated that: "No man, nor number of men upon earth hath power or authority to rule over men's consciences in religious matters." Not only did the plan call for freedom of religion, it stated as basic rights such principles as no taxation without the consent of the taxed, prevention of illegal arrests, and trial by jury. There was confusion over legal ownership of land in the Quakers' New Jersey colony and control eventually went to a group of men belonging to the Church of England. Although the Church of England in New Jersey received certain privileges, there was much tolerance for Protestants of all sects.

William Penn makes a treaty with the Indians to found the Province of Pennsylvania, 1681. Penn obtained the charter for Pennsylvania from Charles II of England in payment of a debt owed to Penn's father.

The details of government he had worked out for West Jersey provided William Penn with valuable experience which he used in founding Pennsylvania in 1681. He started Pennsylvania as a business investment and to conduct a "holy experiment." Penn wanted to prove that liberty and good conduct would result in a satisfying life.

Pamphlets promising religious freedom brought settlers who belonged to many denominations and came from many countries. Under Pennsylvania's Great Law of 1682, no person acknowledging one God was to be penalized in any way because of his religion. Nor could anyone be compelled to attend any religious service not of his own choice.

While Pennsylvania welcomed all faiths, its government resembled that of all other colonies in that it was a Christian government. But it was a Christian government for all Christians. All faiths could worship and all Christians were guaranteed the right to "serve the government in any capacity, both legislatively and executively."

Catholics came to Pennsylvania from the time of its first settlement. During the great English period of intolerance toward Catholics, the British government forced Pennsylvania to pass anti-Catholic laws. Despite these laws, Pennsylvania granted Catholics more religious liberty than they had in any other colony at that time. As the English gradually became less able to exert pressure on the colonies, Catholics in Pennsylvania obtained full freedom of worship.

In Pennsylvania the test of freedom of worship for all was conducted under conditions more difficult than in any other colony. Among the sects which had settled there were Lutherans, Catholics, Jews, Mennonites, Quakers, Baptists, Calvinists, and Episcopalians. In Penn's time there was much trouble among the colonists, and it seemed as if so many denominations could not live together peacefully. But, with the government protecting them all, they learned to live together. Before the end of the colonial period no one could doubt the success of the holy experiment.

PART IV

The Growth of Religious Freedom

At the close of the seventeenth century the cause of religious freedom began to make important gains. In 1689 a Toleration Act was passed in England. The Act did not mark the end of the established church. Nor did it apply to Catholics or Unitarians. But it did grant tolerance, with certain limits, to all other Christians. Although Protestants not belonging to the established church were barred from public office, the Act gave them the right to worship publicly upon registration of their ministers.

As English subjects, the settlers in colonial America expected all rights granted to citizens in England. These rights were not always observed by the rulers in England or by the local colonial lawmakers. However, attempts to deny the liberties granted by the Toleration Act became more and more impossible in the kind of society that had developed in America by the eighteenth century.

1. *The Increased Colonial Population*

With the exception of New England and Virginia, the colonies from their beginnings were populated by more dissenters than members of the established churches. As the population grew, the number of dissenting sects in all colonies increased, as did the number of people in each dissenting sect. No one group was large enough to control every other group within a colony. The English tradition whereby a whole community belonged to a single church could not be kept alive in eighteenth-century America.

A group of Englishmen discuss their plans to make a fortune in the colonies. They usually supported free worship in America in order to attract the settlers necessary to develop the communities.

2. *Freedom and Economics*

For the English government, and for the Englishmen who financed colonial settlements, the colonies were a means of gaining wealth. They favored freedom of worship in America in order to attract the many settlers needed to develop the land and build up trade. When persecuted colonists protested to England, they could usually count on powerful Englishmen to act in their behalf.

Developments in Massachusetts, late in the seventeenth century, illustrate the way dollars and cents, or in this case pounds and shillings, hastened the granting of religious freedom.

A number of very successful Boston businessmen were not members of the established church. They were helping to keep the colony on a firm financial footing, which in turn meant earning a profit for financiers in England. Yet Massachusetts authorities refused when these men demanded the right to vote and to worship in churches of their own. Their situation led to the first major division among Massachusetts Puritans, with one group arguing for greater toleration and another group arguing against it.

In 1686, when the Boston businessmen appealed to England for help, England settled the matter by revoking the Massachusetts charter. Several years later a new charter assured the colonists freedom of worship and extended the right to vote so that it no longer depended on church membership.

Massachusetts is just one example of the way a growing economy helped advance religious toleration throughout America. Warnings from England were not always needed. Farsighted colonists realized that America was a land which offered every advantage — in its climate, its location, and its natural resources — to become a leader in world commerce. To best profit by these advantages, men had to work together and do business with one another in harmony. They knew that an end to religious persecution must come or the great opportunities that America offered would be wasted.

3. *The Spread of New Ideas*

By the middle of the eighteenth century two ideas had become popular enough to influence thinking in favor of tolerance and separation of Church and State.

One was the belief that religion is a personal experience — a matter between the individual and his God. The name of a man's religion wasn't important, but the way his religion influenced his life was.

The second idea was that men have certain natural rights which cannot be taken away by government. Some believed that these rights were given by God. Others believed that they were part of the nature of human beings. Among the most important of these rights was the freedom of the individual to think for himself.

4. *Freedom for a Free Nation*

With the start of the Revolutionary War freedom and liberty were foremost in the minds of all Americans. At first, to many colonists, freedom meant freedom from unfair taxation, and liberty meant the liberties that had been promised Englishmen over the course of many years. In 1776 the colonists decided that these liberties could only be gained by claiming independence from English rule. As the colonies began to organize independent state governments, they had the opportunity to consider many ideas of freedom and liberty. James Madison, Thomas Jefferson, and other outstanding men became the spokesmen for a new kind of freedom that would go far beyond English notions. In ordinary times they would have found it difficult to get their ideas put into law. But these were not ordinary times. Old governments were being changed, and old laws discarded. The pioneers of American liberty were able to bring to their country a plan for a free society where government would exist to serve the people — by working to promote their general welfare, to maintain peace, and to secure justice and liberty for all time to come.

The first blow for liberty. The American Revolution represented freedom in general, not just freedom from British control. Citizens wanted to think for themselves in religious as well as in political matters.

PART V

Heroes, Liberty of Conscience, and Constitutions

1. *Virginia — The Model for Religious Freedom*

The struggle for religious freedom in Virginia has had a major influence on American history. Virginia was the first state to have a written constitution. Its Bill of Rights served as a model for similar bills in other states and for the Bill of Rights adopted by the Federal Government. James Madison's arguments for religious freedom, written during Virginia's first years as a state, are used today when the United States Supreme Court explains its decisions on cases involving the religion clauses of the First Amendment.

Religious leaders, particularly Presbyterian and Baptist, worked to develop the understanding of liberty which became a Virginia tradition. Brilliant Virginia statesmen — James Madison, George Mason, Thomas Jefferson, and Patrick Henry — helped bring full religious freedom to their state and later to the nation.

The Presbyterian minister, Samuel Davies, came to Virginia in the mid-eighteenth century. Preaching in defiance of officials, sending petition after petition to the Virginia legislature and to England, he eventually succeeded in getting Virginia to grant the rights provided by the 1689 English Toleration Act. As a result, many Presbyterians came to Virginia, and their ministers worked for and taught separation of Church and State. Patrick Henry, raised as a member of the Episcopal Church, often attended Presbyterian services. The sermons he heard about the meaning of liberty had a great effect on his life and work. James Madison was also raised as an Episcopalian. But as a student of John Witherspoon, the Presbyterian president of the College of New Jersey, Madison learned Presbyterian ideals of freedom. Witherspoon taught that the use of the words "religious toleration" implies that a group which considers itself superior allows inferior groups to worship.

35

John Witherspoon (1723-1794) and **James Madison** (1751-1836). Witherspoon, a Presbyterian minister who preached religious liberty, saw a place for the clergy in politics. He was one of the signers of the Declaration of Independence and served in the Continental Congress from 1776 to 1782. Madison, as a student of Witherspoon, learned to prefer absolute religious liberty to mere religious toleration.

He told his students that a free society must guarantee not religious toleration but religious liberty — the natural right of each man to worship in his own way, or, if he chooses, not to worship at all. These ideals became Madison's standards. Throughout his many years of service to his country, Madison refused to accept any laws that simply provided toleration — he worked for absolute liberty.

Baptists in Virginia let nothing stop them from preaching in their own manner and from fighting for equality for all faiths. Virginia officials considered the Baptists dangerous fanatics. More than 40 of their preachers were whipped, fined, and sentenced to jail during a period of persecution of Baptists which lasted from 1768 to 1776. Preaching from the windows of their jail cells, the Baptists inspired Virginia champions of freedom to work even harder to secure liberty of conscience for all.

Patrick Henry personally paid the fines of many Baptist preachers. And, as an attorney, he was able to help by defending them in court. When Baptists demanded that they be allowed to preach to their soldiers in the revolutionary army, it was Henry who argued and won their right for them.

In 1776 Virginians met to draw up a constitution under which their government would be ruled as a state. George Mason was chosen to be the author of the Virginia Constitution and Bill of

Both **George Mason** (1725-1792) and **Patrick Henry** (1736-1799) stressed the importance of individual liberties. Together, they opposed the ratification of the Federal Constitution because they felt that it threatened state and personal freedoms. Chiefly through their efforts, a Bill of Rights was added to the United States Constitution.

Rights. The standards for governing Virginia, as set forth by Mason, provided for more freedom and equality than any government had ever granted. Later, as an active participant in the Federal Constitutional Convention, he was able to contribute his ideas to the Constitution and Bill of Rights which would protect the entire American nation.

Patrick Henry worked with Mason in writing the section of the Virginia Bill that stated these principles of religious freedom:

> That religion or the duty which we owe to our Creator, and the manner of discharging it, can be directed only by reason and conviction, not by force or violence; and, therefore, all men are equally entitled to the free exercise of religion, according to the dictates of conscience; and that it is the mutual duty of all to practice Christian forbearance, love and charity towards each other.

The Virginia Bill was a guide for the making of laws which would protect freedom. When members of the Virginia legislature met for the first time under the new constitution, they had to decide what new laws to pass and which old laws to repeal to make the Bill of Rights more than mere words. The Baptists had been petitioning for the abolition of the established church for more than a decade. Now they petitioned again. So did the Presbyterians and Lutherans.

Thomas Jefferson, who by then had become known to all Americans as the author of the Declaration of Independence, left the Continental Congress to join the fight for liberty in Virginia. His task was a difficult one. Although most Virginians by that time belonged to dissenting sects, most members of the legislature belonged to the established church.

Jefferson was only partly successful. He wanted the legislature to pass laws which would guarantee absolute protection of the free exercise of religion and separation of Church and State. The legislators would not go that far. But they did repeal all laws punishing men for their religious beliefs and for not attending church services. Dissenters were exempted from having to pay taxes to support the established church. For members of the established church, there was a temporary exemption from the payment of taxes to support their church. In 1779 this exemption was made permanent.

The majority of Virginians had accepted the idea that government should not levy taxes which would aid one religion only. But in 1784 they were forced to consider if it was a threat to religious freedom for government to levy taxes to aid all religions. Patrick Henry was one of a group of people who believed that religious

Thomas Jefferson (1743-1826) worked for the separation of church and state. In 1786, Jefferson's Bill for Establishing Religious Freedom was passed, making Virginia the first state to grant, by law, full religious freedom.

teaching, by promoting morality and good conduct, helped the state preserve the peace of society. Therefore, this group concluded, all religions should receive tax support. Henry proposed to the legislature a bill requiring an annual tax "for the support of the Christian religion, or of some Christian church, denomination or communion of Christians, or for some form of Christian worship."

James Madison, warning that such a tax levy by the legislature would be a dangerous abuse of power, issued a protest paper which was circulated throughout Virginia.

In this paper, the *Memorial and Remonstrance Against Religious Assessments,* Madison argued that:

(1) Support of religion is a matter of individual conscience. It must be voluntary, not forced.

> ... It is the duty of every man to render the creator such homage, and such only, as he believes to be acceptable to him...

(2) Religion does not need to be supported by law.

> ... the establishment proposed by the bill is not requisite for the support of the Christian religion. To say that it is, is a contradiction to the Christian religion itself; for every page of it disavows a dependence on the powers of this world: it is a contradiction to fact; for it is known that this religion both existed and flourished, not only without the support of human laws, but in spite of every opposition from them...

(3) Taxation for the support of religion endangers liberty.

> ... the proposed establishment ... distant as it may be, in its present form, from the inquisition, it differs only in degree. The one is the first step, the other the last, in the career of intolerance.

(4) Taxation to support religion will make the sects enemies of one another.

> ... it will destroy the moderation and harmony which the forbearance of our laws to intermeddle with religion has produced among its several sects.

Madison's paper, and the petitions against the tax bill which came to the legislature from 48 counties, convinced the legislators that the majority of Virginians believed that support of religion was not the business of government. In 1785 the tax bill was easily defeated. The excitement of the spirit of liberty had taken hold in the Virginia legislature. The lawmakers were finally ready to grant the protection of freedom that Jefferson, Madison, and so many others had long hoped for. Madison asked for consideration of Jefferson's Bill for Establishing Religious Freedom. The bill, which had been introduced in 1779, but never voted on, guaranteed that:

> . . . no man shall be compelled to frequent or support any religious worship, place or ministry whatsoever, nor shall be enforced, restrained, molested or burdened in his body or goods, nor shall otherwise suffer on account of his religious opinions or beliefs, but . . . all men shall be free to profess, and by argument to maintain, their opinions in matters of religion, and that the same shall in no wise diminish, enlarge or affect their civil capacities.

With this bill, passed in 1786, Virginia became the first state to enact into law full religious freedom. Virginia political leaders had worked for 10 years to achieve this freedom. Their next step was to bring its principles into the First Amendment of the Constitution of the United States.

2. *The Constitution of the United States*

A Bill of Rights was not included in the Federal Constitution adopted in 1789. Most of the framers agreed that such a bill was not necessary. They insisted that the government had no powers except those listed in the Constitution.

Those who were worried about freedom of religion were assured that their fears were without reason. The only mention of religion in the Constitution was the statement that: ". . . no religious Test shall ever be required as a Qualification to any Office or public Trust under the United States." Since religion was nowhere else mentioned in the Constitution, the framers explained, the Federal Government could not act upon matters of religion.

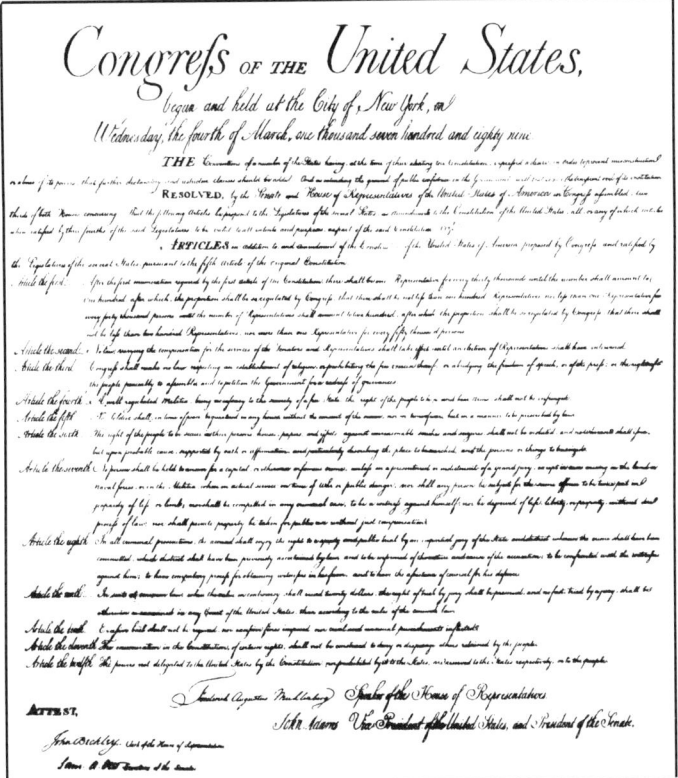

The Bill of Rights became part of the United States Constitution in 1791 when 10 of the 12 recommended amendments were ratified.

State leaders did not agree. Their knowledge of history, and events in their own past, had filled them with a distrust of government. Many ratified the Constitution only after they were promised that the first Congress would amend it to list specific rights with which government could not interfere. James Madison acted at once to draft the amendments desired by the states. Ten of them were ratified in 1791. With the passage of these 10 amendments, known as the Bill of Rights, the American desire for freedom became law.

The First Amendment guarantee of religious freedom, "Congress shall make no law respecting an establishment of religion, or prohibiting the free exercise thereof..." was purposely worded as a double protection. Madison knew that an establishment of religion must be prohibited or religious freedom would never be absolutely safe.

3. Guarantees by the States

By 1789, when the United States Constitution was ratified, 11 of the original 13 states (all except Rhode Island and Connecticut) had adopted constitutions. Virginia, under its constitution and laws, and Rhode Island, under its charter, guaranteed complete freedom of worship and separation of Church and State. The other states, either by their constitutions, or by old laws which were not immediately repealed, had some restrictions pertaining to religion. For example, some required holders of public office to be Christians; some taxed their citizens for the support of religious institutions; and some denied voting rights to Catholics and non-Christians. A number of the states did not allow clergymen to hold public office. The barring of clergymen from government officeholding was considered necessary to keep one denomination from having too much influence. There was also a widespread belief that ministers should not be taken away from their important religious duties.

The passage of the First Amendment did not mean that the states could be forced to provide full religious freedom. The Amendment applied only to Congress. However, the citizens of the states wanted religious freedom. As soon as the First Amendment was passed some states acted to change their constitutions to guarantee full freedom of worship and separation of Church and State. Other states acted more slowly.

By the middle of the nineteenth century the established church in America no longer existed. Every state prohibited taxation for the support of religious institutions. Religious requirements for voting were dropped. Most of the states repealed the law barring ministers from holding public office. (Maryland and Tennessee still prohibit ministers from holding elective office in their state legislatures.) In every state, toleration—meaning *allowing* men of all faiths to worship—had become freedom—recognizing the *right* of men of all faiths to worship.

PART VI

A New Era Begins

1. *Protection of Religious Freedom Extended*

When a lower court hearing brings out a difference of opinion about the constitutionality of a law, the Supreme Court is often called upon to give its judgment. For more than a century after the passage of the First Amendment, the Supreme Court felt it had no authority to judge state laws affecting liberty of conscience.

During the nineteenth century most laws regarding the general welfare of the people were made not by Congress but by the states. Therefore the Court received few cases involving religion, and had little opportunity to study and interpret the protection offered by the First Amendment.

In the twentieth century a number of Supreme Court decisions stated that the First Amendment protection of religious freedom no longer applied only to laws passed by Congress. Branches of state governments were also forbidden to pass laws respecting an establishment of religion or prohibiting the free exercise thereof. The Court used the Fourteenth Amendment (adopted in 1868) as the basis for granting this greater protection. This amendment forbids states to deprive citizens of equal protection of the law, or to deprive them of life, liberty, or property without due process of law.

Twentieth-century Court decisions stated that *liberty* in the Fourteenth Amendment includes both the free exercise of religion and the liberty that would be threatened if an act of government constituted an establishment of religion. These decisions marked the beginning of a new era in the history of religious liberty. For they meant that the nation's highest court could be appealed to by individuals who felt that the actions of any branch of government interfered with liberty of conscience. The Supreme Court had taken upon itself the task of answering the difficult questions raised by attempting to maintain religious freedom in a free society: (1) To what extent can violation of the law be excused to protect the free exercise of religion? (2) What laws are unconstitutional because the interests of society which they protect are not as important as the religious freedom they violate? (3) At what point does government's relationship with religion become an establishment of religion?

2. *How the Supreme Court Operates*

The Supreme Court is made up of nine members — one Chief Justice and eight Associate Justices. There are a few special kinds of cases which originate in the Supreme Court. The majority of cases, however, are appeals for reconsideration of decisions that have been made by state or lower federal courts. The Supreme Court has the privilege of refusing to hear appeals. It only accepts cases which raise important issues of federal constitutional law.

After hearing arguments and studying written statements from lawyers representing each side of an issue, the justices vote to determine a ruling. One of the justices prepares a statement called the opinion of the Court, giving the reasons for the ruling. When all of the justices do not agree, both a majority and a minority, or dissenting, opinion may be prepared. In addition, any justice wishing to add his own views to those expressed in the majority or minority opinions, may write a statement of his own.

The opinions of the Supreme Court help Americans understand the meaning of the Constitution and the Bill of Rights as they apply to the times. Sometimes a ruling is made that reverses an earlier Supreme Court ruling on a similar case. As American ideas of liberty and equality change, new Supreme Court decisions reflect that change.

The Supreme Court of the United States, 1888. This room was originally the Senate chamber. It served the Supreme Court from 1860 until 1935.

PART VII

The Supreme Court Studies the Free Exercise of Religion

1. *Religion and Law — An Early Opinion*

Does the free exercise of religion give an individual the right to break the law?

This question was first answered by the Supreme Court in 1878 in the case of a man who appealed to the Court after having been convicted for being married to more than one woman at the same time.

George Reynolds was a member of the Mormon Church. His religion, at that time, taught that Mormon men, when possible, must practice polygamy or be punished by "damnation in the life to come."

45

George Reynolds, a Mormon convicted for polygamy. In 1878 the Supreme Court upheld his conviction.

(Below) Mormon polygamists. In 1852, Brigham Young, Mormon leader in Utah, formally announced the doctrine of plural marriage for his followers. This statement met widespread antagonism from non-Mormons and led to the imprisonment of many Mormon men. Utah was not allowed to join the Union until the Mormons stated, in 1890, that the practice would be discontinued.

By meeting the requirements of his religion, George Reynolds, and many other Mormons, broke a United States statute which makes bigamy a crime.

In upholding Reynolds's conviction, the Court said: "Laws are made for the government of actions, and while they cannot interfere with mere religious belief and opinions, they may with practices." The Court's opinion spoke of the law against plural marriages and said: "Can a man excuse his practices to the contrary because of his religious belief? To permit this would be to make the professed doctrines of religious belief superior to the law of the land, and in effect to permit every citizen to become a law unto himself. Government could exist only in name under such circumstances."

2. *Religion and Law — The Current Opinion*

In the Reynolds case the Supreme Court stated that the free exercise of religion does not give an individual the right to break the law.

Since then the Court has declared that some laws or government regulations are unconstitutional if they require people to take actions which are forbidden by their religious beliefs. The Court has also declared that some laws or government regulations cannot be enforced if they prevent the free exercise of religion. Some examples of the development of current Court standards are shown in the cases described below.

3. *Compulsory Flag Salute*

Until 1943 school children in many states were required by law to take part in a ceremony in which they saluted and pledged allegiance to the flag. Refusal to participate in these ceremonies meant expulsion from school. In some states the parents of children who refused to salute the flag were subject to criminal prosecution. But to Jehovah's Witnesses, flag salute is forbidden by the Bible. A number of Jehovah's Witness children accepted expulsion from school rather than break the rules of their religion.

School children pledge allegiance to the flag. In 1943, the Supreme Court reversed its previous decision of 1940 by declaring that the compulsory flag salute was unconstitutional.

In 1940 the Supreme Court ruled that compulsory flag salute was not unconstitutional. The Court's opinion declared that: "National unity is the basis of national security... We live by symbols. The flag is the symbol of our national unity, transcending all internal differences, however large, within the framework of the Constitution."

In every society there are some people who will use any excuse to act out their hatred against groups they distrust, disapprove of, or do not understand. The 1940 flag salute decision provided that excuse for many. Over a period of two years after the decision was announced, hundreds of Jehovah's Witnesses were physically attacked. Angry mobs drove some of them out of their homes and forced them to leave the cities in which they lived. In Maine, a Jehovah's Witness church was burned.

On the other hand, there was much criticism of the Court decision in popular magazines, legal journals, and religious publications.

Both types of public reaction influenced the Court. The violence which was touched off by the Court's decision gave the justices good cause to wonder if national unity can, after all, be achieved by symbols. The opinions expressed by judges, lawyers, educators, and representatives of many faiths also affected the thinking of the Court.

In 1943 the Court received another appeal involving compulsory flag salute. Of the eight justices who had voted with the majority in 1940, three said that they had been wrong and two were no longer members of the Court. The 1943 Supreme Court ruling declared that compulsory flag salute is unconstitutional.

Justice Robert H. Jackson, in the Court's majority opinion, said that the freedoms of speech, press, assembly, and worship may be restricted only to prevent grave and immediate danger to interests which the state may lawfully protect. Justice Jackson also said: "... no official, high or petty, can prescribe what shall be orthodox [true] in politics, nationalism, religion, or other matters of opinion, or force citizens to confess by words or act their faith therein..."

Justice Frank Murphy wrote a concurring opinion (an opinion which agrees with the majority). He said that the benefits to society from the compulsory flag salute are not definite enough to justify the invasion of freedom and privacy that is entailed "or to compensate for a restraint on the freedom of the individual to be vocal or silent according to his conscience or personal inclination..."

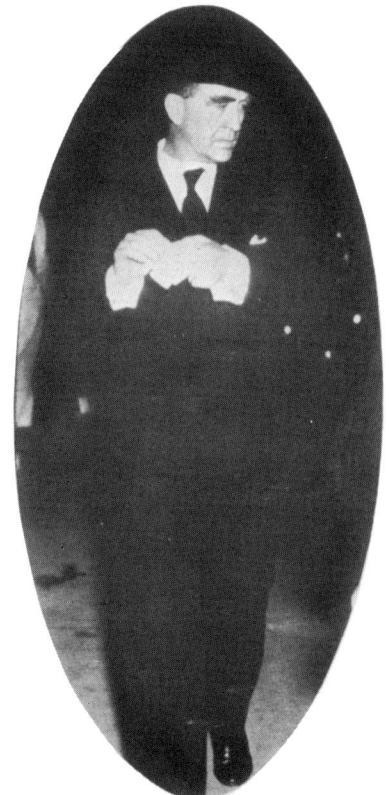

Frank Murphy (1890-1949), Associate Justice of the Supreme Court from 1940 to 1949, was a liberal who felt that the decision to salute the flag should be left to the individual.

4. What Is a Religion?

Can anyone set standards, apply them to each of the hundreds of existing religions, and then say with accuracy, "this one is a religion" but "this one is not"? It would probably be impossible, but government officials often find it necessary to judge whether a group which considers itself a religious body is or is not a religious body. Some circumstances demand that this judgment be made. But in other circumstances, such action by government officials is illegal.

Soliciting Funds for Religious Purposes

Many communities require anyone soliciting contributions for any cause to register with a local official. The official usually investigates to determine whether the cause is being honestly presented to the public. Where such registration is required, solicitors for religious causes are not exempt from it. However, the Supreme Court has ruled that a state authority may not deny anyone permission to solicit funds for religious causes because the authority does not believe the cause is really a religious one.

This decision was made by the Court in 1940, in the case of Cantwell versus Connecticut. Jesse Cantwell, a Jehovah's Witness,

The *Watchtower* and *Awake* are official pamphlets of the Jehovah's Witnesses. Today, any religious group can circulate literature in order to gain aid for its organization.

Jehovah's Witnesses practice mass immersion in New York, 1958. Since the Witnesses consider government to be the work of the devil, they refuse to salute the flag, to bear arms, or to take part in the government.

was attempting to teach his faith by going from house to house selling religious literature. He was arrested and convicted for not first obtaining the license required by Connecticut law. The Court's opinion made it clear that the regulation of solicitation "which does not involve any religious test and does not unreasonably obstruct or delay the collection of funds" is not open to any constitutional objection. The Court explained that: "... a state may protect its citizens from fraudulent solicitation by requiring a stranger in the community, before permitting him publicly to solicit funds for any purpose, to establish his identity and his authority to act for the cause which he purports to represent. The state is likewise free to regulate the time and manner of the solicitation generally, in the interest of public safety, peace, comfort or convenience ..." But the Connecticut law gave the licensing official the power to refuse to grant a license for religious solicitations if he felt the cause was not genuinely religious. On this basis the Court found the Connecticut law unconstitutional and Jesse Cantwell's conviction was reversed. In the words of the Court:

> To condition the solicitation of aid for the perpetuation of religious views or systems upon a license, the grant of which rests in the exercise of a determination by state authority as to what is a religious cause, is to lay a forbidden burden upon the exercise of liberty protected by the Constitution.

Churches and Taxes

The Court, in 1940, said that a state authority cannot determine whether a religious cause is genuinely religious before granting a license to solicit funds. Tax officials, however, face a different problem. They sometimes have to determine whether a claimed religion actually is a religion.

The United States Internal Revenue Service does not tax churches, church schools, or religious groups for the income they receive for religious or charitable purposes. Likewise, individual contributions to religious associations are tax deductible. Most state tax laws provide similar exemptions and deductions.

There are two reasons for the granting of tax exemptions to religious bodies. One is the idea that the power of government to tax gives it the power to control. The other is the fact that nonprofit educational or service organizations (hospitals, symphony orchestras, and art museums, for instance) are not taxed. Churches and religious organizations, since they provide education and perform a public service, are considered part of this tax-exempt group.

A problem arises with the formation of groups that are not directly connected with any religious body already in existence. When these groups consider themselves religious bodies, both state and federal tax officials have the power to decide what, for tax purposes, is a religion. Any group which is denied tax exemption because officials claim they are not a religious body may appeal to the courts.

Draft Exemption for Ministers

Since ministers of religion are exempt from the draft, military draft officials and Justice Department officials sometimes must ask, "What is a religion?" For example, in 1967, Cassius Clay, who was then the world heavyweight boxing champion, refused induction in the armed forces. Clay gave several reasons for his refusal. One was that he is a minister of the Lost Found Nation of Islam (Black Muslim religion), and is, therefore, draft exempt. But draft officials, acting on recommendation of the Department of Justice, refused to grant Clay an exemption. The Department of Justice claimed that the Black Muslim group is a political and racial organization rather than a religious one. Clay, who has taken the name Muhammad Ali, was convicted of draft evasion by a federal jury. He was sentenced to five years in prison and fined $10,000. But the Supreme Court, which overturned the draft conviction in 1971, found that Ali's refusal to serve was actually based on religious beliefs.

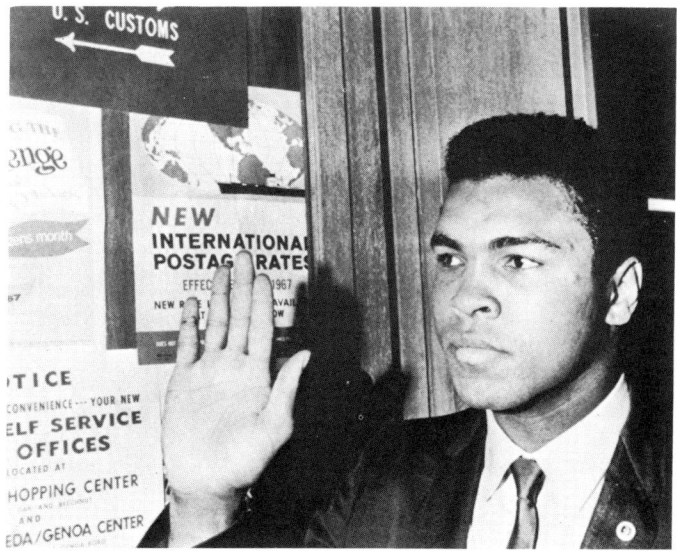

Muhammad Ali received military exemption as a minister of the Black Muslims, even though the Justice Department had claimed that the Muslims were a political rather than a religious organization.

5. *Claims of Religious Experiences*

Individuals may not commit fraud in the name of religion. But can anyone judge whether a claimed religious experience is a fraud?

The Supreme Court had to decide the answer to this question in the 1944 case of the United States versus Ballard. Guy W.,

Edna W., and Donald Ballard, organizers of the *I Am* movement, had been indicted for using the mails to obtain money by false representation. The Ballards had sent out a letter asking for contributions for the *I Am* movement. This letter claimed that Guy Ballard was a divine messenger. It also claimed that the three Ballards had supernatural powers to cure the sick, and that they had already cured hundreds of people. Guy Ballard stated that he had shaken hands with and had talked to Jesus, and that he would pass these conversations on to mankind.

In the opinion of the Court, neither a jury nor any other representative of government can constitutionally decide whether alleged religious experiences did or did not occur. Solicitation for money, based on a claimed religious experience, is fraudulent only when the prosecution can prove that the solicitors do not honestly believe in the claims they make. In the words of the Court:

> Men may believe what they cannot prove. They may not be put to the proof of their religious doctrines or beliefs. Religious experiences which are real as life to some may be incomprehensible to others. Yet the fact that they may be beyond the ken of mortals does not mean that they can be made suspect before the law. Many take their gospel from the New Testament. But it would hardly be supposed that they could be tried before a jury charged with the duty of determining whether those teachings contained false representations.

Mrs. Edna Ballard and her son **Donald,** organizers of the *I Am* movement, were convicted of dishonestly using the mail to obtain money. The Supreme Court reversed their conviction.

6. Religious Requirements for Public Officeholding

As previously noted, the Constitution states that "no religious Test shall ever be required as a Qualification to any Office or public Trust under the United States." Nevertheless, as late as 1960, Maryland and six other states required individuals to acknowledge their belief in a Supreme Being before they could hold public office. The question of the constitutionality of these requirements came to the Supreme Court in 1961. The Court was appealed to by a resident of Maryland whom the Governor had appointed to the office of notary public. When the appointee refused to swear that he believed in the existence of God, he was not allowed to take his appointed position.

The Supreme Court ruled that the Maryland religious test for public office violates both of the religion clauses of the Constitution. When the Supreme Court ruled the Maryland test unconstitutional, similar tests in other states automatically became unconstitutional.

7. Free Exercise of Religion — How the Court Determines Limits

As the twentieth-century Supreme Court received case after case concerning the free exercise of religion, it developed standards by which to judge these cases. These standards recognize the duty of government to pass laws which protect the interests of our society. A law can never be passed for the purpose of limiting the free exercise of religion. However, when an otherwise valid law has the incidental effect of restricting the free exercise of religion, the Court asks: Is the interest of society which the law protects important enough to warrant restriction of religious freedom? When a majority of justices answer no, the law may be declared unconstitutional.

When an individual is convicted for actions performed as a result of his religious beliefs, the court asks: Did the action of the individual present a grave and immediate danger to interests which the state may lawfully protect? If a majority of the Court answers no to this question, the conviction is likely to be overruled.

Associate Justice **Tom Clark** served on the Supreme Court from 1949 to 1967.

This particular test of the Court is often used in cases where the "action" involved is constitutionally protected by the right of free speech. It would apply, for example, in the instance of a minister whose sermons attack other religions.

Supreme Court Justice Tom Clark summed up the purpose of the Free Exercise Clause with these words:

> The Free Exercise Clause . . . withdraws from legislative power, state and federal, the exertion of any restraint on the free exercise of religion. Its purpose is to secure religious liberty in the individual by prohibiting any invasions thereof by civil authority.

PART VIII

The Supreme Court Studies the Establishment Clause

1. *What Does the Establishment of Religion Clause Mean?*

In the 1947 case of Everson versus Board of Education the Supreme Court began a thorough study of the meaning and purpose of the words, "Congress shall make no law respecting an establishment of religion . . . ."

Justice Hugo L. Black, writing for the Court, summarized the arguments made by James Madison in the *Memorial and Remonstrance Against Religious Assessments* and quoted from Thomas Jefferson's Bill for Establishing Religious Freedom.

Justice Black said that "the provisions of the First Amendment, in the drafting and adoption of which Madison and Jefferson played such leading roles, had the same objective and were intended to provide the same protection against governmental intrusion on religious liberty" as Thomas Jefferson's Bill.

The establishment of religion clause of the First Amendment, according to Justice Black, means that:

- Neither a state nor the Federal Government can set up a church.
- Neither can pass laws which aid one religion, aid all religions, or prefer one religion over another.
- Neither can force nor influence a person to go to or to remain away from church against his will or force him to profess a belief or disbelief in any religion.
- No person can be punished for entertaining or professing religious beliefs or disbeliefs, for church attendance or nonattendance.
- No tax in any amount, large or small, can be levied to support any religious activities or institutions, whatever they may be called, or whatever form they may adopt to teach or practice religion.

- Neither a state nor the Federal Government can, openly or secretly, participate in the affairs of any religious organizations or groups and vice versa.
- In the words of Jefferson, the clause against establishment of religion by law was intended to erect "a wall of separation between Church and State."

A majority of Supreme Court justices have consistently agreed with Justice Black's statement of the meaning and purpose of the First Amendment guarantee against an establishment of religion by government. But agreement as to the meaning and purpose of the Establishment Clause does not insure that all of the justices will agree on a decision in any particular case.

2. An Establishment of Religion— How the Court Decides

Every case arising under the Establishment Clause involves the question of government aid to religion. This aid might come about in two ways. The first is through the passage of laws, rules, or regulations which assist one or several religions to spread their doctrines. A requirement that public schools start their day with the recitation of a prayer would be in this category. The second aid to religion occurs through the use of government funds to benefit one or all religious institutions. A government grant of funds to build a Sunday School building would be an example of this type of aid.

To determine whether laws falling within these categories constitute an establishment of religion, the Court asks: What is the purpose or the main effect of the law? If either the purpose or the main effect is to help or harm religion, the law violates the Establishment Clause of the First Amendment.

Government means any branch of government. A state legislature is a branch of government. So is a school board. These two branches of government, in the past, have been involved in most of the Establishment cases coming to the Supreme Court.

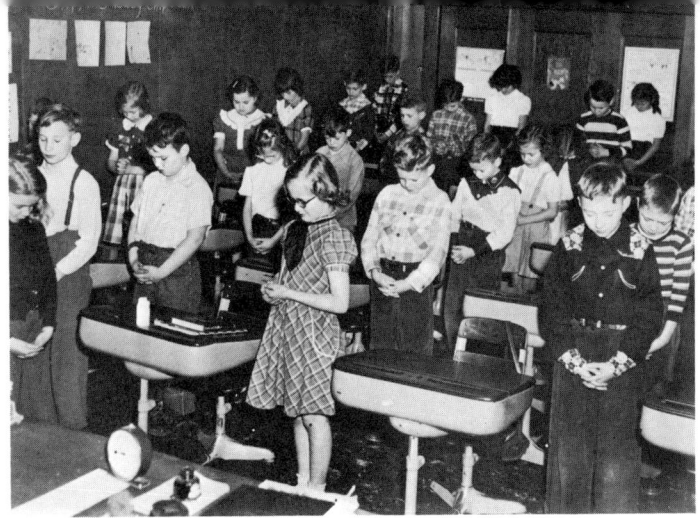

Silent prayer in a public school. Many persons classify school prayer as government aid to religion. The topic has been debated many times in the Supreme Court.

3. Why Does the Court Say "Government Can Not Aid Religion"?

Most Supreme Court justices, and many religious and political leaders, feel that government should not aid religion. Those who hold this point of view believe that government aid to religion or to religious institutions threatens religious freedom. They reason that:

(1) When government passes laws to help religions spread their teachings, the views of the most powerful religions will be forced on all others.

(2) Support of religion by government, whether it is financial support or support by government sponsorship of prayer, weakens religion. Religion can be truly strong only when prayer and support of religious institutions are voluntary.

(3) Religion is a matter of individual liberty. If government undertakes its support, it may then undertake its regulation and individual liberty would be lost.

(4) Religious schools are private schools. Their main purpose is to teach religion. If this were not their main purpose, most students now attending religious schools would attend public schools. Private organizations cease to be private when they receive government support.

4. *The Argument for Government Aid to Religion or Religious Schools*

Some Supreme Court justices, and religious and political leaders, feel that government should aid religion or religious institutions as long as they do not prefer one religion over another. Their reasoning is:

(1) Religious institutions perform valuable public services. They support many hospitals, nursing homes, homes for the aged, schools, and welfare and counseling agencies. If religious groups did not support these facilities it is very likely that many of them would have to be supported by the government.

(2) In 1967, six million American children attended church-related schools. These schools, in addition to teaching religious doctrine, provide their pupils with a general education. They meet state educational requirements. Therefore, any government aid to education which is offered to public schools should also be offered to religious schools. Any government public welfare assistance offered to public school children (free lunches, special remedial classes, free bus transportation) should also be offered to children attending religious schools. To deny aid to education and public welfare assistance to children attending church schools would be punishing those who exercise their religious freedom by attending religious rather than secular schools.

(3) We are a religious nation and many of our customs are of religious origin. If government cannot promote or sponsor interfaith religious activities, American life may become emptied of traditions that have been part of our society for generations.

5. *Disagreement Among Supreme Court Justices*

Although a majority of justices on the Supreme Court have agreed that government may not directly aid religion, there has been much disagreement about some kinds of government laws or regulations which indirectly aid religion. The problems faced by the justices, as they attempt to decide what kind of government aid is constitutionally permissible, are shown in the cases which follow.

PART IX

Aid to Parochial School Children

1. *The New Jersey Bus Fare Case*

Is a law permitting the use of tax money for transportation of children to Catholic parochial schools a help to religion? Or is it part of general welfare legislation intended to help all school children?

This was the question considered by the Court in the 1947 case of Everson versus Board of Education. According to New Jersey law, local school boards could repay parents for money they spent to send their children to and from school on public buses. Part of this money went to parents whose children attended Catholic parochial schools. The Supreme Court was asked if the use of tax money to pay for transportation to parochial schools violates the First Amendment guarantee against an establishment of religion.

The Court, by a five-to-four vote, ruled that the First Amendment does not prohibit New Jersey "from spending tax-raised funds to pay the bus fares of parochial school pupils as part of a general program under which it pays the fares of pupils attending public and other schools."

A protest march in Florissant, Missouri. An estimated 500 citizens demonstrated against a decision by the legislature to reject bus service for private and parochial school students.

The majority and minority opinions in this case illustrate how members of the Court can be in complete agreement about the basic meaning of the Establishment Clause, yet differ in their opinions of the constitutionality of a particular law.

Justice Black, in presenting the majority opinion, listed the limitations imposed by the First Amendment ban against an establishment of religion by government. These limitations are quoted in this book on pages 57 and 58.

Justice Black then examined the New Jersey law in view of these limitations, and said: "...we must not strike that state statute down if it is within the state's constitutional power *even though it approaches the verge [limit] of that power*...New Jersey cannot consistently with the 'establishment of religion' clause of the First Amendment contribute tax-raised funds to the support of an institution which teaches the tenets and faith of any church." However, in the opinion of the majority, the New Jersey law does not contribute money to the parochial schools. It is public welfare legislation which "does no more than provide a general program to help parents get their children, regardless of their religion, safely and expeditiously to and from accredited schools."

The majority opinion further said that since the law providing government support for transportation of all school children is public welfare legislation, New Jersey cannot exclude children from receiving its benefits "because of their faith or lack of it."

Justice Black concluded:

> The First Amendment has erected a wall between Church and State. That wall must be kept high and impregnable. We could not approve the slightest breach. New Jersey has not breached it here.

The opinion of the minority was prepared by Justice Wiley B. Rutledge and supported by three other justices. The minority opinion included a full printed text of James Madison's *Memorial and Remonstrance Against Religious Assessments*. The minority drew its conclusions as to the constitutionality of the New Jersey

Hugo L. Black (1886-1971) was an Associate Justice of the Supreme Court from 1937 to 1971. Though he had been a member of the Ku Klux Klan for a brief period, Justice Black worked hard in defense of civil liberties and was known as a "militant humanitarian." It is said that Justice Black carried a copy of the Constitution with him continually. He was especially concerned that church and state be strictly separated.

law from the principles stated in Madison's *Memorial*. The majority also used the ideals presented in Madison's *Memorial*, both in listing the limitations imposed on government by the First Amendment, and in other parts of the opinion. The minority agreed with Justice Black's list of limitations. But to their way of thinking, these limitations prohibit financing of transportation of parochial school children even when it is part of a program which pays for the transportation of all school children. The minority opinion said:

> Does New Jersey's action furnish support for religion by use of the taxing power? Certainly it does, if the test remains undiluted as Jefferson and Madison made it, that money taken by taxation from one is not to be used or given to support another's religious training or belief, or indeed one's own... Here parents pay money to send their children to parochial schools and funds raised by taxation are used to reimburse them. It aids them in a substantial way to get the very thing which they are sent to the particular school to secure, namely, religious training and teaching.

In the opinion of Justice Rutledge, the cost of transportation is as much a part of the cost of education as any of the other expenses of providing and receiving education. The opinion suggested that if a law which allows government to finance transportation to religious schools is public welfare legislation for the purpose of promoting education, and "the Amendment's force can be thus destroyed...there could be no possible objection to more extensive support of religious education by New Jersey."

Justice Rutledge also said:

> Education which includes religious training and teaching, and its support, have been made matters of private right and function not public, by the very terms of the First Amendment. That is the effect not only in its guaranty of religion's free exercise, but also in the prohibition of establishments. It was on this basis of the private character of the function of religious education that this Court held parents entitled to send their children to private, religious schools...Now it declares in effect that the appropriation of public funds to defray part of the cost of attending those schools is for a public purpose. If so, I do not understand why the state cannot go farther or why this case approaches the verge of its power.

2. *Textbook Loans to Parochial School Children*

After the Everson case, the issue of government aid to church school children was not ruled on by the Supreme Court until 1968. The textbook loan case was brought to the Court by two local boards of education in New York State. It involved a New York law which requires public school boards to buy and to supply textbooks, without charge, to all children residing in the school districts who are enrolled in grades seven to twelve of a public or private school. Parochial (church-related) school children are included. The books are loaned to the children who use them for their classwork but do not keep them. While the texts used by church school children are legally owned by public boards of education, they may be stored on the premises of the religious school. The choice of the books used by a church-related school is made by the individual parochial school heads, but each book ordered must be approved by the public school authorities and only nonreligious books may receive approval.

The Supreme Court, in a six-to-three decision, ruled that the New York law in question does not violate the Constitution. Justice Byron R. White, in writing the Court's majority opinion, used the test which asks if the purpose or the main effect of a law is to help or harm religion. The Court concluded that the purpose of the New York law is to aid the educational opportunities available to the young. In the opinion of the majority, the books are furnished to the pupils, not to the schools, and the financial benefit is to parents and children, not to schools.

Justice Hugo Black, in a dissenting opinion, called the New York law a "flat, flagrant, open violation of the First and Fourteenth Amendments which together forbid Congress or state legislatures to enact any law respecting an establishment of religion." In comparing this case with the Everson ruling (p. 61), Justice Black declared that there is a great difference between "books, which are the heart of any school," and "bus fares, which provide a convenient and helpful general public transportation service." Justice Black further said:

> ... It requires no prophet to foresee that on the argument used to support this law others could be upheld providing for state or government funds to buy property on which to erect religious school buildings or to erect the buildings themselves, to pay the salaries of the religious school teachers, and finally to have the sectarian religious groups cease to rely on voluntary contributions of members of their sects while waiting for the Government to pick up all the bills for the religious schools... I still subscribe to the belief that tax-raised funds cannot constitutionally be used to support religious schools, buy their school books, erect their buildings, pay their teachers, or pay any other of their maintenance expenses, even to the extent of one penny. The First Amendment's prohibition against governmental establishment of religion was written on the assumption that state aid to religion and religious schools generates discord, disharmony, hatred, and strife among our people.... And I still believe that the only way to protect minority religious groups from majority groups in this country is to keep the wall of separation between Church and State high and impregnable as the First and Fourteenth Amendments provide.

PART X

Religious Instruction During Public School Hours

1. *Released Time for Religious Instruction in a Public School*

In 1948, a year after the Supreme Court decided the Everson case, it examined the Establishment Clause as it applied to a new problem. This case, McCollum versus Board of Education, involved religious instruction in the public schools of Champaign, Illinois.

The religious classes were held once a week, during school hours, for pupils whose parents had given permission for their children to participate. The classes were taught in the regular schoolrooms. Students who did not take the instruction were sent to other rooms where they did their usual classwork. Students who were released from their studies for religious instruction were required to be present at the religious classes. These classes were taught by instructors whose salaries were paid by a voluntary interfaith group, the Champaign Council on Religious Education. There was no cost to the state, but the instructors had to be approved by the superintendent of schools.

Mrs. Vashti McCollum, the mother of one of the Champaign students, brought suit to prohibit the religious instruction program.

The opinion of the Court, delivered by Justice Black, ruled the Champaign released time program unconstitutional. Only one justice dissented.

Mrs. Vashti McCollum objected to the use of public school time and facilities for religious instruction. The Supreme Court supported her opinion.

Justice Black pointed out that tax-supported property was being used for religious instruction, and that there was close cooperation between the school authorities and the religious council in promoting religious education. He said:

> The operation of the state's compulsory education system thus assists and is integrated with the program of religious instruction carried on by separate religious sects. Pupils compelled by law to go to school for secular education are released in part from their legal duty upon the condition that they attend the religious classes. This is beyond all question a utilization of the tax-established and tax-supported public school system to aid religious groups to spread their faith. And it falls squarely under the ban of the First Amendment (made applicable to the States by the Fourteenth) as we interpreted it in Everson versus Board of Education.

2. *Released Time for Religious Instruction Given Outside the School*

In 1952 the Court was again faced with the issue of released time for public school children to receive religious instruction. In Zorach versus Clauson the Court considered a New York program which permitted public schools to release students from classes to receive religious instruction away from school. Students were released upon written request from their parents. Those who were not released stayed in the classrooms. Attendance reports were sent to the schools so they could make sure that children who had been released had reported for religious instruction.

The Court majority declared that the New York program did not violate the First Amendment. In the opinion written by Justice William O. Douglas, the Court stated:

> We are a religious people whose institutions presuppose a Supreme Being. We guarantee the freedom to worship as one chooses...We sponsor an attitude on the part of government that shows no partiality to any one group and lets each flourish according to the zeal of its adherents and the appeal of its dogma. When the state encourages religious instruction or cooperates with religious authorities by adjusting the schedule of public events to sectarian needs, it follows the best of our traditions... To hold that it may not would be to find in the Constitution a requirement that the government show a callous indifference to religious groups. That would be preferring those who believe in no religion over those who do believe...[The government] can close its doors or suspend its operations as to those who want to repair to their religious sanctuary for worship or instruction. No more than that is undertaken here.

Justice Douglas said that this case is unlike McCollum versus Board of Education:

> In the McCollum case the classrooms were used for religious instruction and the force of the public school was used to promote the instruction. Here...the public schools do no more than accommodate their schedules to a program of outside religious instruction. We follow the McCollum case. But we cannot expand it to cover the present released time program unless separation of Church and State means that public institutions can make no adjustments of their schedules to accommodate the religious needs of people. We cannot read into the Bill of Rights such a philosophy of hostility to religion.

Supreme Court Justice **William O. Douglas.**

Justices Hugo L. Black, Felix Frankfurter, and Robert H. Jackson each wrote separate dissenting opinions.

In the opinion of Justice Black:

> Except for the use of the school buildings (in McCollum versus Board of Education) there is no difference between the systems which I consider even worthy of mention. In the New York program, as in that of Illinois, the school authorities release some of the children on the condition that they attend the religious classes, get reports on whether they attend, and hold the other children in the school building until the religious hour is over... The sole question is whether New York can use its compulsory education laws to help religious sects get attendants presumably too unenthusiastic to go unless moved to do so by the pressure of this state machinery. The state thus makes religious sects beneficiaries of its power to compel children to attend secular schools. Any use of such coercive power by the state to help or hinder some religious sects or to prefer all religious sects over nonbelievers or vice versa is just what I think the First Amendments forbids. In considering whether a state has entered this forbidden field the question is not whether it has entered too far but whether it has entered at all. New York is manipulating its compulsory education laws to help religious sects get pupils. This is not separation but combination of Church and State.

Robert H. Jackson (1892-1954) was an Associate Justice of the Supreme Court from 1941 to 1954. He was a strong defender of religious freedom.

Justice Frankfurter wrote:

Of course a state may provide that the classes in its schools shall be dismissed, for any reason, or no reason, on fixed days, or for special occasions. The essence of this case is that the school system did not "close its doors" and did not "suspend its operations." There is all the difference in the world between letting the children out of school and letting some of them out of school into religious school classes. If everyone is free to make what use he will of time wholly unconnected from schooling required by law...then of course there is no conflict with the Fourteenth Amendment.

Justice Jackson's dissent stated:

If public education were taking so much of the pupils' time as to injure the public or the students' welfare by encroaching upon their religious opportunity, simply shortening everyone's school day, would facilitate voluntary and optional attendance at church classes...As one whose children, as a matter of free choice, have been sent to privately supported church schools, I may challenge the Court's suggestion that opposition to this plan can only be antireligious, atheistic, or agnostic. My evangelistic brethren confuse an objection to compulsion with an objection to religion...We start down a rough road when we begin to mix compulsory public education with compulsory godliness.

PART XI

Prayer and Bible Reading in Public Schools

1. *The New York Regents' Prayer Case*

A 1962 Supreme Court decision set off a storm of controversy so great that the President of the United States was asked to issue a public statement and a number of individuals wanted to change the First Amendment. The case under consideration, Engel versus Vitale, is often referred to as the Regents' Prayer Case.

The New York Board of Regents, which governs the state's public schools, composed this prayer: "Almighty God, we acknowledge our dependence upon Thee, and we beg Thy blessings upon us, our parents, our teachers, and our country." The Regents recommended that the prayer be recited each morning in New York public schools.

Bertram Daiker (left) and **William J. Butler** (right), the lawyers in the Regents' Prayer Case, reargue the case for law students. The case involved the use of a prayer in the public schools. Butler claimed that the particular prayer had been state-composed and compulsory. Daiker claimed that "there is nothing in the record that says the prayer was state-composed."

Not all of New York's local school boards acted upon the Regents' recommendation. The Board of Education in New Hyde Park was one which did.

The parents of 10 pupils challenged the constitutionality of the use of this prayer as part of public school procedure. In 1962 the Supreme Court ruled that the New York program of daily recitation of the Regents' prayer was unconstitutional. Justice Hugo L. Black delivered the opinion of the Court. He said: ".... the constitutional prohibition against laws respecting an establishment of religion must at least mean that in this country it is no part of the business of government to compose official prayers for any group of the American people to recite as a part of a religious program carried on by government.... There can be no doubt that New York's state prayer program officially establishes the religious beliefs embodied in the Regents' prayer."

The Board of Education had defended the use of the Regents' prayer by saying it was non-denominational and that its recitation was voluntary. Children who objected to reciting the prayer were allowed to remain silent or could, if they wished, leave the room. To this Justice Black replied that the ban on establishment of religion by government "is violated by the enactment of laws which establish an official religion whether those laws operate directly to coerce nonobserving individuals or not."

In the opinion of the Court, the first and most immediate purpose of the Establishment Clause rested on the belief that a union of government and religion tends to destroy government and to degrade religion. "Another purpose of the Establishment Clause," noted Justice Black, "rested upon an awareness of the historical fact that governmentally established religions and religious persecutions go hand in hand."

The Court's opinion made it clear that the ruling in this case did not indicate hostility to religion:

> It has been argued that to apply the Constitution in such a way as to prohibit state laws respecting an establishment of religious services in public schools is to indicate hostility toward religion or toward prayer. Nothing, of course, could be more wrong . . . there were men of . . . faith in the power of prayer who led the fight for adoption of our Constitution and also for our Bill of Rights with the very guarantees of religious freedom that forbid the sort of governmental activity which New York law has attempted here. These men knew that the First Amendment which tried to put an end to governmental control of religion and of prayer, was not written to destroy either. They knew rather that it was written to quiet well-justified fears which nearly all of them felt arising out of an awareness that governments of the past had shackled men's tongues to make them speak only the religious thoughts that government wanted them to speak and to pray only to the God that government wanted them to pray to. It is neither sacrilegious nor antireligious to say that each separate government in this country should stay out of the business of writing or sanctioning official prayers and leave that purely religious function to the people themselves and in those the people choose to look to for religious guidance.

Justice Black's opinion concluded with a response to those who might think the Regents' prayer too brief and general to be considered dangerous:

> It may be appropriate to say in the words of James Madison, the author of the First Amendment: "It is proper to take alarm at the first experiment on our liberties. Who does not see that the same authority which can establish Christianity, in exclusion of all other Religions, may establish with the same ease any particular sect of Christians, in exclusion of all other Sects? That the same authority which can force a citizen to contribute three pence only of his property for the support of any one establishment, may force him to conform to any other establishment in all cases whatsoever?"

Supreme Court Justice **Potter Stewart.**

Two justices did not participate in this case. Justice Potter Stewart was the only dissenter. In his minority opinion he stated that he did not see how an official religion "is established by letting those who want to say a prayer say it. On the contrary, I think that to deny the wish of these school children to join in reciting this prayer is to deny them the opportunity of sharing in the spiritual heritage of our Nation."

2. *Daily Bible Reading and Recitation of the Lord's Prayer*

In 1963, one year after it had delivered the Regents' Prayer decision, the Supreme Court considered two additional cases involving religious exercises in public schools. The Court made one ruling which applied to both cases.

The facts of School District versus Schempp

Pennsylvania law required that each public school day be opened with the daily reading, without comment, of 10 verses from the Bible. Any child could be excused from participating in the Bible reading, or could leave the room, upon written request from his parents.

At Abington Senior High School, the Bible passages were read by selected students and were broadcast into each homeroom through an intercommunication system. This was followed by the recitation of the Lord's Prayer, also broadcast through the inter-

The Schempp family stands before the Supreme Court Building in Washington. The Schempps objected to Bible readings in the public schools, as the passages often conflicted with their Unitarian beliefs. Most Unitarians believe that God is a single being.

communication system. Students in the classrooms were asked to stand and join in repeating the prayer in unison. The student reading the Bible verses could select the passages he wanted to read. While students were permitted to read from any version of the Bible, the school furnished only the King James (Protestant) version.

Mr. and Mrs. Edward Schempp, whose children attended the Abington school, brought suit to determine the constitutionality of the Pennsylvania law. The Schempps testified that some of the religious doctrines, as read from the Bible, were contrary to the beliefs and teachings of their Unitarian faith. The Schempps did not want their children excused from the room because they felt that this would affect their relationship with their teachers and with other students.

The facts of Murray versus Curlett

Under a rule adopted in 1905 by the Board of School Commissioners of Baltimore, Maryland, opening exercises in the city's schools consisted of the reading, without comment, of a chapter from the Bible. The rule provided that the Lord's Prayer could be used with the Bible reading or in its place.

Mrs. Madalyn Murray, and her son William J. Murray III, were professed atheists. William was a student in a Baltimore public school.

Mrs. Murray and her son filed suit to have the Baltimore religious exercises declared unconstitutional.

The Court ruled that religious exercises, when conducted as part of the curricular activities of public school students, violate the Establishment Clause of the First Amendment.

Justice Tom Clark, who delivered the Court's opinion, said that the fact that individual students could be excused from participating in the exercises cannot be used as a defense. The exercises themselves constitute an establishment of religion. Justice Clark added: "Further, it is no defense to urge that the religious practices here may be relatively minor encroachments on the First Amendment. The breach of neutrality (by government) that is today a trickling stream may all too soon become a raging torrent."

Justice Clark emphasized that by not permitting a state to require religious exercises, even with the consent of the majority of those affected, the Court is not denying the majority's right to free exercise of religion. "While the Free Exercise Clause clearly prohibits the use of state action to deny the rights of free exercise to anyone, it has never meant that a majority could use the machinery of the State to practice its beliefs."

Justice Clark, in the above statement, was pointing out that everyone has the right to worship according to his own beliefs. People may worship in their homes, in their churches, and in many other places. But state laws — in this case state laws requiring school attendance — may not be used by any group to establish its religion.

Mrs. Madalyn Murray is an atheist who protested religious readings in the public school that her son attended. Her beliefs disclaim the existence of any God.

Former President of the United States, **John F. Kennedy** (1917-1963). After the ruling on the Regents' Prayer Case, he reminded Americans that prayer could still have prominence in the home.

3. *Reaction to the Court's Ban on Religious Exercises in Public Schools*

The Supreme Court ruling in the Regents' Prayer Case was handed down on June 25, 1962. A majority of the public reacted with anger. Some religious leaders denounced the ruling as shocking and frightening. One member of Congress called it the most tragic decision in the history of the United States; another said it was a blow to all believers in a Supreme Being.

Others accepted the decision, and some praised it. President John F. Kennedy, at a press conference on June 27, 1962, said:

> We have in this case a very easy remedy, and that is to pray ourselves, and I would think that it would be a welcome reminder to every American family that we can pray a good deal more at home and attend our churches with a good deal more fidelity, and we can make the true meaning of prayer much more important to the lives of all our children.

While the Court was considering the Schempp-Murray cases, spokesmen for several major religious groups declared their opposition to the holding of religious observances in public schools. When the Court announced its decision in June of 1963, the reaction was different from what it had been a year earlier. Many publicly criticized the Court's ruling. But the majority either accepted or approved of it.

4. *Attempts to Change the First Amendment*

After the Supreme Court rulings in the prayer and Bible reading cases, more than 100 congressmen introduced measures to amend the Constitution. These measures would reword the First Amendment to permit Bible reading and recitation of prayers in public schools. Those who favored changing the First Amendment said that they wanted to regain the free exercise of religion which the Court had taken away.

During 1963 and 1964 Congress held public hearings on the proposed changes. Constitutional authorities, and leaders of religious organizations representing all faiths, came to these meetings to speak against altering the First Amendment. As the proposals were discussed and debated it became clear that there was no way to reword the Amendment without a resulting loss of liberty. The First Amendment remained unchanged.

5. *Public Opinion After 1964*

There are some schools which continue to hold religious exercises contrary to the Supreme Court ruling. This practice will go on as long as no protest is raised by the parents of children attending the schools in which the exercises are held. The majority of schools, however, have accepted the Supreme Court decisions, as have a majority of the general public.

In 1968 the Supreme Court received one more appeal on the issue of prayer in public schools.

Even though the Supreme Court has ruled against it, many schools continue to hold religious services.

The appeal came about as the result of a "thank-you verse" which was recited by kindergarten children in De Kalb County, Illinois, each day before they had their morning snack. The wording of the verse was:

> We thank you for the flowers so sweet;
> We thank you for the food we eat;
> We thank you for the birds that sing;
> We thank you for everything.

The parents of one of the kindergarten children sued to have the compulsory recitation of this verse declared unconstitutional.

The Seventh United States Circuit Court of Appeals said that the verse is as harmless as anything can get so far as imposing religious tenets upon nonbelievers. Nevertheless, the court declared that the verse is a prayer, and as such comes within the Supreme Court decisions banning prayer in public schools.

The ruling of the circuit court was appealed to the United States Supreme Court. On January 22, 1968, the Supreme Court announced that it upheld the lower court ruling that the "thank-you verse" is a prayer and cannot be recited as part of a public school's daily procedure.

The Court's ruling that there should be no prayer in public schools had been so well accepted by then that there was no general public reaction to the announcement of the 1968 decision.

Felix Frankfurter was an Associate Justice of the Supreme Court from 1939 to 1962. He was a liberal, but he believed that the court must exercise restraint in interfering with popular sentiment.

6. *Church and State — The Court's Dilemma*

The phrase "separation between Church and State" was first used by Thomas Jefferson in a letter written in 1802 to the Danbury Baptists Association. Jefferson wrote:

> Believing with you that religion is a matter which lies solely between man and his God, that he owes account to none other for his faith or his worship, that the legislative powers of government reach actions only, and not opinions, I contemplate that act of the whole American people which declared that their legislature should "make no law respecting an establishment of religion, or prohibiting the free exercise thereof," thus building a wall of separation between Church and State.

Many Supreme Court decisions refer to "a wall of separation between Church and State." These words have provided the Court with no ready-made answers. The Court's dilemma was expressed by Justice Felix Frankfurter with these words:

> We are all agreed that the First and the Fourteenth Amendments have a secular reach far more penetrating in the conduct of Government than merely to forbid an "established church." But agreement, in the abstract, that the First Amendment was designed to erect a "wall of separation between Church and State," does not preclude a clash of views as to what the wall separates.

PART XII

Conclusion

1. *The Free Exercise of Religion*

Religious Freedom and Freedom of Speech

In many circumstances the free exercise of religion is protected not only by the rights to worship and believe but also by the constitutional guarantee of freedom of speech. Religious rights which involve speech are, therefore, highly protected. They assure each individual the freedom to express his religious beliefs and to work to spread those beliefs in many ways, as, for example, by preaching sermons; by writing letters, books, and articles; and by making speeches. Religious beliefs may be freely expressed whether they are conventional ones which are acceptable to most people or unusual ones that many might object to.

Any individual may preach or use written religious material in order to solicit money for a religious cause. A government official may not refuse to permit the solicitation of funds because he does not believe the cause is a genuinely religious one.

Similarly, any individual may, by speaking or writing, describe a personal religious experience. If the claimed experience is used as the basis for raising funds for a religious cause, government officials may not judge whether or not the experience actually occurred. Fraudulent collection of money could be charged only if a court could prove that the individual did not honestly believe that he had had the experience.

Along with the freedom to state and teach religious doctrine is the right to hear or to refuse to hear such doctrine. Church attendance or nonattendance is strictly a matter of individual conscience — it may never be demanded by laws. Religious worship or teachings may not be conducted in a public school where children have come to receive a secular (nonreligious) education. On the other hand, parents may not be denied the right to send their children to church-related schools so long as those schools meet state educational requirements.

Freedom of religion is illustrated by the wide variety of religious magazines published and circulated throughout the United States. Catholics and Jews, as well as Protestants, publish many magazines.

Finally, government may never force anyone to profess a religious belief which he does not hold. Government may not demand that any person declare a belief in a specific religion or in religion in general in order to vote or to hold public office.

Religiously Required Conduct

Laws are made for the protection of society, and religious freedom does not automatically give an individual the right to break the law in order to perform a religious duty. When a religion requires its members to perform acts which are in violation of state or federal law, government officials sometimes decide if the violation presents an important threat to the interests of society. In cases where such a decision must be made, officials weigh the needs of society which the law in question protects against the need of the individual for religious freedom. If the need of the individual for religious freedom is found to be greater, he might be excused from the conditions of that law.

2. An Establishment of Religion

In interpreting the constitutional ban against an establishment of religion by government, the justices of the Supreme Court have repeatedly stated that government can neither help nor harm religion. In fact, however, government does sometimes help religion. The rulings of the Supreme Court on establishment cases indicate that, in the Court's opinion, some kinds of help are constitutionally permissible while other kinds are prohibited. Since the Court did not directly deal with establishment cases until 1947, there are only a few absolute statements that can be made about the kinds of government help to religion which are or are not in violation of the First Amendment.

Government Aid in the Spreading of Religious Beliefs

The government has made it very clear that religious training or worship in public schools is unconstitutional. Religious exercises, such as devotional Bible reading or the recitation of prayers, may not be conducted in a public school as part of the school program. Religious instruction for public school children is also banned when that instruction is given on the school property. However, public school children may be excused from classes to attend religious instruction which is conducted by private groups away from school property.

Direct Financial Aid to Religion

No branch of government can give direct financial aid to any religious institution to use for purely religious purposes. For example, government may not pay ministers' salaries, give a religious group the funds with which to build a church, or supply religious institutions with free Bibles.

Indirect Financial Aid to Religion

Indirect financial aid to religious institutions is one of the most controversial of all problems falling under the Establishment Clause. The extent to which the government may provide financial aid which indirectly benefits religion has not been made clear by Court decisions. The problem is especially difficult when it involves general welfare legislation which benefits school children —both those who attend public schools and those who attend church-related schools.

In 1947, the Supreme Court upheld a New Jersey law which permitted government payment for bus transportation to parochial school children as part of a general program which financed bus transportation for all school children. At that time the Court suggested that the New Jersey legislature, in passing this law, was approaching the limits of its power. In 1968, however, the Court upheld a New York law which required local public school boards to purchase textbooks to supply on loan to parochial school students. This law, also, is part of general welfare legislation. It provides textbooks for all school children. As in its 1947 ruling, the Court stated that the New York law benefits children and their parents, not the religious schools.

The Supreme Court's ruling on the New York law came during a period of great national concern with improving conditions for the poor, the undereducated, and all other minority groups. It implies that the current attitude of the Court is that general welfare legislation, which meets important local or national needs, may be found constitutionally permissible even when the incidental benefit to a religious institution is great.

United States stamp of 1957 commemorating the Flushing Remonstrance. In 1657, Governor Peter Stuyvesant of New Amsterdam proclaimed that Quakers and non-Quakers remain separate. The citizens of Flushing protested by signing the Flushing Remonstrance, the first citizen declaration of religious freedom.

...INDEX...

atheists *7,75,76*

Ballard, Edna and Donald *53,54*
Baptists *16,17,24,25,30,35-37,80*
Bay Psalm Book, The 17
Bill for Establishing Religious Freedom *38,40,57*
Bill of Rights, U.S. *35,37,40,41, 44,68,73*
Bill of Rights, Virginia *35-37*
Black, Hugo L. *57,58,62,63,65-67, 69,72,73*
Black Muslims *53*
bus fare aid *61-64,83,84*
Butler, William J. *71*

Calvert, Cecil *19-21*
Calvert, George *19*
Calvinists *30*
Cantwell, Jesse *50,51*
Cantwell vs. Connecticut *50,51*
Catholics *7,16,18-21,30,31,61-65,82*
Church of England *15,16,21,22,28,29*
claims of religious experience *53,54,81*
Clark, Tom *56,76*
Clarke, John *25*
Clay, Cassius (see Muhammad Ali)
Congregationalists *16*
Constitution, U.S. *37,40-42,44,73*
Cotton, John *16*

Daiker, Bertram *71*
Davies, Samuel *35*
De Kalb County case *78,79*
Douglas, William O. *68,69*
draft exemption *52,53*

Engel vs. Vitale (see Regents' Prayer Case)
Episcopalians *15,30,35*
Establishment Clause *13,57-80, 82-84*
Everson vs. Board of Education *57,61-65,67*

First Amendment *7,8,13,40-43,57, 58,61-65,67-69,71,73,78,80*
flag salute *47-49*
Flushing Remonstrance *84*
Fourteenth Amendment *43,65, 67,70*

Fox, George *26,27*
Frankfurter, Felix *69,70,80*
Free Exercise Clause *13,45-56,81,82*

Henry, Patrick *35-39*

I Am movement *54*

Jackson, Robert H. *49,69,70*
James II, King of England *21*
Jefferson, Thomas *34,35,38,40, 57,63,80*
Jehovah's Witnesses *47-49,50,51*
Jews *7,8,12,24,30,82*

Kennedy, John F. *77*

Lutherans *30,37*

Madison, James *34-36,39-41,57, 62,63,73*
Maryland *19-21,55*
Maryland Toleration Act *20,21*
Mason, George *35-37*
Massachusetts Bay Colony *16-18, 22,23,32,33*
McCollum, Mrs. Vashti *66,67*
McCollum vs. Board of Education *66-68*
Memorial and Remonstrance Against Religious Assessments 39,40,57,62,63
Mennonite Amish *9-11,30*
Mormons *45-47*
Muhammad Ali *52,53*
Murphy, Frank *49*
Murray, Madalyn *75,76*
Murray vs. Curlett *75,76,78*

Penn, William *26,28-30*
Pennsylvania *29,30*
persecution *7,8,12,16,17,20,21, 26-28,36,48*
Pilgrims *6,18*
Plymouth Colony *6,18*
polygamy *45-47*
Presbyterians *35-37*
Protestants *7,15,18-20,26,29,31,82*
Providence (see Rhode Island)
public office, religious test for *55*
Puritans *16,17,20-23,32*

Quakers *7,16,17,24-30*

85

Regents' Prayer Case *71-74,77*
released time *66-70,83*
Revolutionary War *34*
Reynolds, George *45-47*
Rhode Island *24-26,42*
Roth, Lawrence *14*
Rutledge, Wiley B. *62-64*

St. Luke's Church *15*
Schempp family *75*
School District vs. Schempp *74,75,78*
school prayer *58,59,71-80,83*
Second Baptist Meetinghouse *25*
soliciting funds *50,51,81*
Stewart, Potter *74*
Stone, William *20*
Supreme Court *11,43-84*

tax exemption *52*
taxpayer's suit *14*
textbook loans *64,65,84*
Toleration Act of 1689 *18,31,35*

Unitarians *20,31,75*
U.S. vs. Ballard *53,54*

Virginia *15,16,35-40,42*

West Jersey *28,29*
White, Byron R. *65*
Williams, Roger *22-26*
Winthrop, John *16*
Witherspoon, John *35,36*

Young, Brigham *46*

Zorach vs. Clauson *67-69*

ACKNOWLEDGMENTS

The illustrations are reproduced through the courtesy of: pp. 6, 16 (left), 18, 29, 34, 37 (left), 38, 41, 45, Library of Congress; p. 7, Philosophic Library, Inc.; p. 8, Crown Publishers; pp. 9, 10, 11, Charles S. Rice; p. 12, Photo by Milton J. Blumenfeld; pp. 14, 19, 21, 22, 23, 24, 27 (top and bottom), 28, 32, 49, 50, 56, 69, 70, 80, Independent Picture Service; p. 15, Virginia Chamber of Commerce, Photo by Phil Flournoy; pp. 16 (right), 20, 36 (left and right), 37 (right), *Dictionary of American Portraits*, Dover Publications, Inc.; p. 17, Courtesy of the Rare Book Division, New York Public Library, Astor, Lenox and Tilden Foundations; p. 25, American Press; p. 46 (top and bottom), Utah State Historical Society; pp. 48, 53, 59, 61, 67, 71, 75, 79, Religious News Service Photo; p. 51. *Watch Tower Bible and Tract Society of Pennsylvania*; p. 54, Wide World Photos; p. 63, Harris and Ewing; p. 74, Yale University Library; p. 76, *Baltimore News American*; p. 77, Democratic-Farmer-Labor Party; p. 82, *Christian Herald*; p. 84, Post Office Department, Division of Philately.

ABOUT THE AUTHOR...

RAVINA GELFAND graduated from the University of Minnesota where she studied English, journalism, and psychology. She also did postgraduate work in English and writing at both the University and Macalester College. A former weekly newspaper editor, she has written for radio and magazines. She is the co-author of *They Wouldn't Quit: Stories of Handicapped People* and the author of *The Freedom of Speech in America*. She and her husband live in Minneapolis with their two sons.

The IN AMERICA *Series*

The AMERICAN INDIAN *in America*
The CHINESE *in America*
The CZECHS & SLOVAKS *in America*
The DUTCH *in America*
The EAST INDIANS & PAKISTANIS *in America*
The ENGLISH *in America*
The FRENCH *in America*
The GERMANS *in America*
The GREEKS *in America*
The HUNGARIANS *in America*
The IRISH *in America*
The ITALIANS *in America*
The JAPANESE *in America*
The JEWS *in America*
The MEXICANS *in America*
The NEGRO *in America*
The NORWEGIANS *in America*
The POLES *in America*
The PUERTO RICANS *in America*
The RUSSIANS *in America*
The SCOTS & SCOTCH-IRISH *in America*
The SWEDES *in America*
The UKRAINIANS *in America*
The FREEDOM OF THE PRESS *in America*
The FREEDOM OF RELIGION *in America*
The FREEDOM OF SPEECH *in America*

We specialize in publishing quality books for young people. For a complete list please write:

LERNER PUBLICATIONS COMPANY
241 First Avenue North, Minneapolis, Minnesota 55401